A TROJAN WOMAN

Sara Farrington

A version of
THE TROJAN WOMEN
by Euripides

BROADWAY PLAY PUBLISHING INC
New York
www.broadwayplaypublishing.com
info@broadwayplaypublishing.com

Cover photo: Stephanie Gamba, SMPhotos

First edition: May 2024
This edition, revised: January 2026
I S B N: 979-8-88856-012-9

Book design: Marie Donovan
Page make-up: Adobe InDesign
Typeface: Palatino

PLAYWRIGHT'S NOTE

A TROJAN WOMAN exists inside an act of modern warfare. I was originally inspired by an early moment in the Russian war against Ukraine that affected me deeply. Ukrainian civilians Tetiana Perebyinis, 43 and her two kids, Mykyta, 18 and Alisa, 9, were killed as they fled on foot from their suburb of Irpin to Kyiv. The moment was photographed by Lynsey Addario of The New York Times and came to represent Russian brutality upon Ukrainian civilians.

But, of course, my version of the Euripides fits inside any conflict in any country in any time period, from the Peloponnesian War and the massacre at Melos, which Euripides was protesting with this play, to today.

The ancient Greek part of this play exists inside that moment of attack and THE CIVILIAN's realization of it, beginning on "This is Troy" and ending on "Exit the Chorus."

The stage can be covered floor to ceiling in the debris and wreckage of modern war or completely bare but for the essentials listed.

I would like to thank Meghan Finn who trusted me with "any Greek play you want," Drita Kabashi who journeyed the globe to perform this role, Ioli Andreadi and Aris Asproulis who welcomed us to their glorious city of Athens, Ari Laura Kreith who brought us home to NJ.

I am also so grateful for the intrepid spirit and support of Carol Ostrow and Stop The Wind Theatricals who continue to hold high the torch of this beautiful piece.

And of course thanks to Reid Farrington for his continued unpaid role as my consigliere.

A TROJAN WOMAN is dedicated to my two sons, Jack and Levi.

NOTE ON MUSIC

For performance of copyrighted songs, arrangements or recordings referenced in this play, permission of the copyright owner(s) must be obtained. Other songs, arrangements or recordings may be substituted provided permission from the copyright owner(s) of such songs, arrangements or recordings is obtained, or songs, arrangements or recordings in the public domain may be substituted.

A TROJAN WOMAN was commissioned by The
Interbalkan Festival of Ancient Drama of Athens
(Artistic Director: Aris Asproulis) and presented at
Theatro Attikou Aldous/Katina Paxinou Attica Grove
Theater in Athens, Greece, 5 July 2023. The cast and
creative contributors were as follows:

THE CIVILIAN .... Drita Kabashi

Director .... Meghan Finn
Production Manager .... Hanna Yurfest
Greek Translator .... Ioli Andreadi
Videographer/Editor .... Ana Veselic
Film Producer .... Jessica Chermayeff
Costumes .... Suzanne Bocanegra

A TROJAN WOMAN premiered in the US at Luna Stage, NJ (Artistic Director: Ari Laura Kreith) as a co-production with The Tank NYC (Artistic Director: Meghan Finn) 15 March 2024. The cast and creative contributors were as follows:

THE CIVILIAN .... Drita Kabashi

Understudy .... Madelyn Robinson
Director .... Meghan Finn
Lighting Designer ....David Heguy
Production Manager ....Lucas Pinner
Stage Manager ....Ian Sanchez
Costumes .... Suzanne Bocanegra

CHARACTERS

This piece is performed by one woman, THE CIVILIAN, *a mother, aged anywhere between 30-50.*

THE CIVILIAN *embodies every character in* THE TROJAN WOMEN *with the help of the physical markers listed below:*

POSEIDON: *Half a bottle of water.*

ATHENA: *A long metal pipe.*

QUEEN HECUBA: *A round, plastic laundry basket, usually held over her head, cage-like.*

CHORUS: *Two umbrellas.*

TALTHYBIUS: *A clipboard with papers and a stool to stand on.*

CASSANDRA: *A camping lantern.*

ANDROMACHE: *A small folding stroller.*

MENELAUS: *A damaged bike helmet.*

HELEN OF TROY: *A length of chain.*

Hector's shield is represented by a garbage can lid.

THE CIVILIAN'*s son is represented by a child sized bright blue puffer coat.*

(*At rise:*)

(THE CIVILIAN *cautiously walks onstage, pushing a stroller. Strapped in the stroller is a bright blue child's puffer winter coat. She herself wears the same style coat, only bright pink.*)

(THE CIVILIAN *walks the entire perimeter of the stage, over and over, throughout the opening speech. The stroller is always in front of her, until noted.*)

THE CIVILIAN:
They won't kill civilians.
They won't kill civilians.
They said take this evacuation route across the bridge to the city where it's safe.
They don't kill civilians.
(*Beat*)
I shouldn't have put this off for so long.
I shouldn't have hidden in the apartment so long.
I should have left a long time ago but he's only seven.
Why am I doing this with a seven year old?
It's fine, it's fine, they don't kill civilians, they don't kill civilians.
(*She picks up the pace.*)
Why am I doing this with a seven year old?
I'll tell you why, girl, tanks rolled through your neighborhood, that's why.
Right past your building, that's why.
Why am I walking out into the open air?
It's fine, it's fine.

(*A sound of war is heard.* THE CIVILIAN *is now walking very, very quickly.*)

THE CIVILIAN:
He called last night, my love, my life, fighting on the
front as all men are, as all men should.
"We're leaving in the morning," I said. "They said it
was safe, they said we could leave."
"No you're not!" He said.
"Yes we are," I said. "We'll be fine," I said, "we'll make
it."
"Oh yeah?" He was angry. "What makes you so sure?"
He growled.
"Because they don't kill civilians."
How many times do I have to explain it?
(Now she is jogging.)
We'll be fine, we'll be fine, we'll be fine, we'll be fine.
Me and my little man in his puffy bright blue winter
coat.
"You're gonna wear this when we leave, honey," I
explained, "so I can spot you!"
"Then you have to wear yours!" He pointed to my
puffy bright *pink* winter coat.
"So I can spot *you*!" he said.
*(Now she is running, propelling the stroller along the
perimeter of the stage.)*
We'll make it, we'll make it, we'll make it, we'll make
it.
We'll make it to the bridge, we just need to get across
the bridge to the city.
It's okay it's okay it's okay it's okay it's okay it's okay.
"I'm gonna carry you now, okay? Like when you were
a little baby!"
*(She unclicks her "child" or rather, the bright blue coat, and
carries him as she runs, leaving the stroller behind.)*
We don't need to run, we don't need to run, we don't
need to run.
From what? From who?
We are clearly civilians and they don't kill civilians.
(She runs as fast as she can run now.)

If only I could get to that bridge—!
If only I hadn't left our apartment—!
If only I hadn't wheeled in that *fucking wooden horse*—!

(*A massive "explosion" and* THE CIVILIAN *and the bright blue puffy winter coat are thrown to the ground and all across the stage.*)

(*A silence*)

(*Soon,* THE CIVILIAN *rises, disoriented.*)

(*She removes her pink coat, trance-like, dropping it. She is now dressed in the shredded rags of ancient Troy.*)

THE CIVILIAN:
This is Troy!
These crumbling ruined walls, this tangle of debris is Troy!
Troy has been rendered thusly because Troy has just lost a war against Greece.
That war, even though Greece started it, ended it and won it,
is called The *Trojan* War.
It doesn't make sense! I know!
But if you are looking for sense,
Perhaps we are not the species for you.

(THE CIVILIAN *locates and presents a plastic laundry basket. This is* QUEEN HECUBA.)

THE CIVILIAN:
Enter Hecuba, Queen of Troy.
Former Queen of Troy.
The matriarch of the Trojan royal family.
Mother to nineteen children, all but one, dead.
(*Beat*)
Is a mother still a mother if all her children are dead?
If not, what is she?
Just a woman again?
Just a woman.

Spared to live out her days as that filthy old bag
shackled to the radiator in the kitchen corner peeling
potatoes.
Queen Hecuba, whose feet, once, never touched the
floor.
Queen Hecuba?

(QUEEN HECUBA *turns, slow and labored, to look at* THE
CIVILIAN, *hangs there a moment, before collapsing to the
stage—or rather dropped.)*

THE CIVILIAN:
We'll let her be for now.
Enter Poseidon.

(THE CIVILIAN *locates a discarded half-filled bottle of water.
This is* POSEIDON.)

THE CIVILIAN:
Poseidon, presiding over the oceans, weather and
waves.
Poseidon, moody, like the seas he dictates.
Devastated one day, amorous the next,
Icy-cold today, flirty-sexy tomorrow,
Rageful now, but later known to whisper, "my love,
my life, my love, my life…"
What mood grips Poseidon in this moment?
Oh Poseidon?

(POSEIDON *is markedly depressed in voice and body. He has
a surfer dude vibe.)*

POSEIDON:
Hey.

THE CIVILIAN:
Hi. Are you okay?

POSEIDON:
Not really.
Just here visiting my city of Troy for the final time.

THE CIVILIAN:
Your city?

POSEIDON:
Oh yeah, I built Troy myself.
I sculpted it delicately with water and time.
I crashed over it and over it and over it…
I loved Troy, I really did, I had such a great *vision* for it:
an azure paradise at the edge of the earth.
A resort town, you know?
But then, the Greeks came. The Greeks, the Greeks.
And honestly, it could have gone either way for a
while there—Troy could have won, truly she really
could have!
Until that horse.

THE CIVILIAN:
Horse? What horse?

POSEIDON:
That horse.
Crafted by Athena herself.
Gifted oh so delicately at Troy's doorstep,
like a casserole to a sick aunt.

THE CIVILIAN:
Yeah? Go on. Then what happened?

POSEIDON:
Eh.
Someone else will have to explain it to you, I'm too
depressed.
My Troy, my Troy is…
Do you know what *keening* is?

THE CIVILIAN:
Keening? No, I don't think so.

POSEIDON:
It's a *sound*, hard to describe exactly.
It's this grotesque, prolonged wail of just…

well,
pure concentrated *grief*.
THE CIVILIAN:
Like this?

(THE CIVILIAN *keens in a very real way. The agony of the
immediate aftermath of the opening explosion breaks through
for a moment.*)

POSEIDON:
Yeah that's it, that's Troy, alright.
Where there was music, keening.
Where there was laughter, keening.
Dance? Keening.
Theater? Keening.
Art, food, drink, sex?
Keening, keening, keening, *keening*.
See those women over there?

(THE CIVILIAN *locates and opens two umbrellas, holding
one in each hand. This is the* CHORUS.)

(CHORUS 1 *and 2 unleash another peel of keening*)

POSEIDON:
Those are the *women* of Troy.
Although, honestly, you can't really call them women
anymore.
Women have, like, bodies and brains and opinions and
stuff, right?

THE CIVILIAN:
That's right.

POSEIDON:
Well these don't.
They're *lots*.
Just waiting there to see who gets to be whose slave in
Greece.

THE CIVILIAN:
Slave?

POSEIDON:
Yeah, you know—sex slave, kitchen slave, wife slave,
child slave—whatever.
And—oh. Look. It's Hecuba.
Just collapsed on the ground there.
She was a queen only yesterday it seems.
Now she's a *lot* too.
I don't even think she cares *what* she is at this point,
would you?
She's lost everyone.
Her husband Priam,
all her children but one.

THE CIVILIAN:
Which one?

POSEIDON:
Cassandra, of course.
Her other daughter Polyxena, she's dead too, although
Hecuba doesn't know that yet, so shh, for now.
And Cassandra may as well be dead after what she's
been through.

THE CIVILIAN:
What's she been through?

POSEIDON:
Eh,
I'm too depressed to talk about it.
Between you, me and the seven wives of Zeus,
Cassandra's a little—

(THE CIVILIAN *sloshes the water around in the bottle in a
circular motion.*)

POSEIDON:
And now with Cassandra going off to become
Agamemnon's sex slave?
I mean, there's not a lot there in the way of
psychological tranquility.

THE CIVILIAN:
Agamemnon?

POSEIDON:
King of Greece? Head of the House of Atreus?
It's hard to keep it all straight, I know, even I struggle.
What was I saying?

THE CIVILIAN:
Hecuba? You asked if I lost everything, would I care
what happened to me?

POSEIDON:
Would you?

THE CIVILIAN:
No. I wouldn't.

POSEIDON:
Yeah, so.
Anyway, are we done here? I gotta get going.
It's kind of *awkward* for the gods in Troy now.

THE CIVILIAN:
Why's it awkward for the gods in Troy?

POSEIDON:
Honestly I have no idea.
I slap around here like I always have, but lately I get
the strangest feeling I'm not welcome?
Any ideas why that might be?

THE CIVILIAN:
Well, let's see.
Did you help them?

POSEIDON:
Did I help who?

THE CIVILIAN:
The *Trojans*.

POSEIDON:
What do you mean?

THE CIVILIAN:
I mean when one human was slitting the throat of
another human—another member of their own species
— did any gods reach down from Mount Olympus and
flick the murderer into the ocean? Straighten things
out? Isn't that what gods are for?

POSEIDON:
I'm not sure I understand the question?

THE CIVILIAN:
Did no god intervene?

POSEIDON:
Um…no?

THE CIVILIAN:
Why not?

POSEIDON:
We just didn't.

THE CIVILIAN:
But why? *Why?!*

POSEIDON:
(Suddenly rageful, larger than life, terrifying)
Why?
Why?
WHY?!
BECAUSE!
THAT'S WHY!
(Small beat and he's calm again.)
Anyway, I'm taillights, okay?

(THE CIVILIAN *locates a long metal pipe, reminiscent of a
spear, and holds it firmly. This is* ATHENA.)

ATHENA:
Poseidon!

THE CIVILIAN:
Hold on: Enter Athena.

Gray-eyed Athene, bright-eyed Athene!
Ergane! Athena the craftswoman, designer of wooden horses.
Nike! Athena the great warrior, leveler of Troy.

ATHENA: *(In a state of shock)*
Poseidon…

POSEIDON:
Athena. Great.
What do you want?

ATHENA:
Oh gods, gods…

POSEIDON:
What are you Oh gods-ing about, *you won,* Athena!
Troy is gone, you scorched the earth! You're victorious!

ATHENA:
I just…

POSEIDON:
You just…?

ATHENA:
I just saw…

POSEIDON:
You just saw what?

ATHENA: *(Horrified)*
Ajax.

POSEIDON:
Ajax? So what?
He's your fearless Greek warrior, you see him all the time.

ATHENA:
I saw Ajax…*defiling* my temple.

POSEIDON:
What do you mean, *defiling*?

ATHENA:
Cassandra—
She was running for her life and…
…took refuge in my temple in the center of the city of
Troy.
Sought sanctuary at my feet.
And though I know you judge me now as bloodthirsty,
vengeful, competitive and vain—
But in that moment, I thought only to offer her peace in
my house.
But in that moment,
Ajax.
I watched as Cassandra heard the clap of his heels in
my house, approaching behind her.
I watched as Cassandra's head shot up, pleading eyes
to me: don't let him, don't let him, don't let him!
I watched as she slowly turned, saw Ajax towering
over her and scurried to her feet.
I watched as Ajax pushed her body against my stone
legs.
I watched as he overtook her, forced himself in her as
she shrieked in pain.
I watched as he finished, cast her down in a heap and
chuckled on his way out.
No one defiles my temple and gets away with it.
That kind of hubris must be paid for.

POSEIDON: (*Getting interested*)
Agreed.
What are you thinking?

ATHENA:
I'm thinking in your infinite control over the sea, my
dear friend, might I call in a favor?

POSEIDON:
I'm listening.

ATHENA:
Could I trouble you to make it a really, *really* rough journey home for the Greek army?

POSEIDON: *(Considering, then getting into it)*
Pummeling rain?

ATHENA:
Hurricanes?

POSEIDON:
Squalls?

ATHENA:
HA HA! Know your place, you prideful mortals!

THE CIVILIAN:
STOP!

POSEIDON:
What?

ATHENA:
What?

(Small beat)

THE CIVILIAN:
How can you gods switch so easily between love and hate?

ATHENA: *(To* POSEIDON*)*
Who is this person?

POSEIDON:
She's a civilian.
You ready?

ATHENA:
Always. Let's teach those Greek boys some manners.

THE CIVILIAN:
Exit the gods.

(THE CIVILIAN *tosses the water bottle and spear/pipe.* THE
CIVILIAN *then goes to* HECUBA, *collapsed on the ground.
She delicately lifts* HECUBA *half way up.)*

THE CIVILIAN:
Do you need help, Queen Hecuba?

HECUBA:
No, no, leave me here.
I want to lie here.
Until my body breaks down
and becomes a part of the ground.
And one day,
many years from now,
people will dance on me,
not knowing.
But until then,
I'll ride the next wave of grief to the shore,
swim back out,
then ride the one after that.
What else is there to do?
My home is gone.
My husband is gone.
My children are gone.
My ancestral line, gone.

THE CIVILIAN:
Queen Hecuba—-

HECUBA:
Queen? I am queen of nothing.

THE CIVILIAN:
Oh, well, Hecuba then, I was wondering if you could
tell me why?
Why did the Greeks destroy Troy?
There must be a very good reason.

HECUBA:
Why else? A *woman*! One woman.
She's back there now,

hiding.
I KNOW YOU'RE THERE, *WOMAN!*
(She finally stands.)
It's a good thing you're hiding, a good thing for you!
Because if there's *one thing* that would give me merciful respite from this unbearable grief,
one thing I could actually continue to *live* for—
it would be to beat you to death with my bare hands!

(THE CIVILIAN hoists the CHORUS.)

THE CIVILIAN:
Enter Chorus!

CHORUS 1:
Oh Queen Hecuba! What will happen to us now?

CHORUS 2:
We've heard such horrible rumors!

CHORUS 1:
What will happen? What will happen?

CHORUS 2:
Will we be slaves?

CHORUS 1:
Will we be sacrificed?

CHORUS 2:
We heard about bondage—

CHORUS 1:
We heard about torture—

CHORUS 2:
—kidnappings!

CHORUS 1:
—hard labor!

CHORUS 1:
Will I ever see my home again?
My parents?
My brothers?

CHORUS 2:
My lovers and friends?

HECUBA:
I don't know and I'm not your queen and all those
things are dead!

CHORUS 1:
Maybe it won't be so bad!

CHORUS 2:
Sure!
Greeks can't *all* be bad!

CHORUS 1:
I've met some pretty okay Greeks!

CHORUS 2:
Maybe my new Greek master will be handsome and
sweet!

CHORUS 1:
A poet, a playwright, a painter!

CHORUS 2:
I'll become his captive muse!

CHORUS 1:
And you know, I've heard Etna's not so bad,
maybe I'll be taken there!

CHORUS 2:
There's another place I've heard of, I can't remember
the name,
on the Ionian Sea?

CHORUS 1:
Oh I know it!
With water so purifying you become a year younger
with every swim?

HECUBA:
Fools!

You'll be chained to some vengeful Greek's bed by
sundown.

THE CIVILIAN:
Hecuba?

HECUBA:
What?

THE CIVILIAN:
Let them lie to themselves.

HECUBA:
Why?

THE CIVILIAN:
Allow them a fantasy world to retreat to, if only for a
moment.

HECUBA:
A fantasy world, of course.
I believe some cultures call it "hope."

CHORUS 1:
Look!

CHORUS 2:
Who comes?

CHORUS 1:
A messenger?

CHORUS 2:
Yes!
A herald from the Greek army!

(THE CIVILIAN *drops the* CHORUS *umbrellas and removes
the* HECUBA *crown and drops it, indicating that* HECUBA
has again collapsed.)

THE CIVILIAN:
Enter the messenger Talthybius!
Eternal bearer of bad news.

(THE CIVILIAN *locates and presents a broken clipboard overflowing with fluttering papers and a stool to stand on. This is* TALTHYBIUS. *He is a pencil pusher, a middle manager, a slave to policy, the "I was only taking orders" type. He speaks like a customer service agent reading from a script.*)

TALTHYBIUS:
Hello and good morning how are we today? Good!
Glad to hear it.
My name is Talthybius and I'll be your herald from the
Greek army.
Who might I be speaking with this morning?

HECUBA:
Queen Hecuba.

TALTHYBIUS:
Good morning Miss Hecuba, how are you today?

HECUBA:
Queen Hecuba.

TALTHYBIUS:
Good morning Miss Queen Hecuba, how are you
today?

HECUBA:
Ruined.

TALTHYBIUS:
Good! Glad to hear it.
I've come with some very good news for you.
The Greeks have drawn their lots.

(THE CIVILIAN *shoves* TALTHYBIUS *under her armpit and grabs both broken umbrellas for the* CHORUS.)

(CHORUS *1 and 2 keen like wailing police sirens.*)

TALTHYBIUS:
We do appreciate your concern and we assure you
we're here to answer all your questions.

(THE CIVILIAN *grabs the crown for* HECUBA.)

HECUBA:
Cassandra, my poor unraveled daughter, who gets
her?

TALTHYBIUS:
Please give me a moment of your time while I look that
up for you.

(TALTHYBIUS *hums a few bars of the telephone hold music
version of* The Girl From Ipanema *until he "returns".*)

TALTHYBIUS:
We thank you for your patience.
We have some very good news for you regarding your
daughter Cassandra.
She has been selected by none other than *King
Agamemnon* himself.
Isn't that wonderful?
She's going to be a king's *mistress.*
You should be very proud, Miss Queen.

HECUBA:
Oh my unhappy child…
And my younger daughter?
Polyxena?
My little girl, my little baby…
What happens to her?

TALTHYBIUS:
Please give me a moment of your time while we look
that up for you.

(TALTHYBIUS *hums the same telephone hold music until he
"returns".*)

TALTHYBIUS:
Miss Hecuba, I do have an answer for you regarding
the fate of a *Polyxena,*
I am happy to report that you no longer have to worry
about Polyxena.

HECUBA:
What do you mean? Speak plainly!

TALTHYBIUS:
We hear that you are dissatisfied, Miss Queen Hecuba
and encourage you to report all service complaints by
calling the Greek army at—

HECUBA:
I beg of you, speak!

TALTHYBIUS:
Polyxena has been given the wonderful job of watching
over the tomb of Achilles!

HECUBA:
Watching over his tomb?
She's just going to sit there?

TALTHYBIUS:
We do appreciate your question.
You see, sometimes young virgin girls are called upon
to *watch* over the grave of great powerful Greek men.
And although young Polyxena felt a *slight pinch* in the
moment of her job offer,
we are happy to report she is now completely pain-
free.
And for her work,
she will make the great Achilles a very, very happy
ghost.

HECUBA:
Then…she lives?

TALTHYBIUS:
Uh…in our hearts.

HECUBA:
Small mercies, small mercies.
And my daughter-in-law, Andromache?

TALTHYBIUS:
Andromache, Andromache…

THE CIVILIAN:
One moment—
Andromache: Wife to Queen Hecuba's son Hector, the
great Trojan warrior killed by Achilles with a knife to
the throat.
To the outside eye, she was only the unnamed good
wife and mother.
Good nose, good breasts, good eyes, good brows, good
hair, good neck, good cheeks, good wit, good listener.
See? Good.
No name needed.
But to me, Andromache is…
Andromache is…Andromache…is…

(THE CIVILIAN *goes to the blue puffer coat for the first time
since the top. She keens for a moment, again the real world
crashing in briefly.*)

(*She soon goes back to the play.*)

HECUBA:
What of Andromache!?

(*Again,* TALTHYBIUS *hums telephone hold music until he
"returns".*)

TALTHYBIUS:
Wonderful news for you, Miss Queen Hecuba,
Miss Andromache has been assigned to the great
Achilles' son, Neoptolemus!
Surely you know him!
Portly teenager? Flaming red hair? Murdered your
husband Priam?

HECUBA:
Oh.
Of course. Neoptolemus.
She'll be thrilled.
And…me?
Old woman that I am.
Unable to stand, unable to walk,

gnarled fingers, gnarled toes,
blind with grief and rage.
Who desires to own a bag like me?

TALTHYBIUS:
We ask for a moment of your time.

(*Again* TALTHYBIUS *hums telephone hold music, but
"returns" quickly this time—this answer comes easy.*)

TALTHYBIUS:
We appreciate your patience and you'll be pleased to
know we do have an answer for you, Miss Queen.
As of sundown tonight,
you will be the official state property of the great and
powerful…*OOOOOdysseus!*
(*Long silence*)
Miss Queen?

HECUBA:
Vile fiend.

TALTHYBIUS:
We hear your concerns but—

HECUBA:
Lying bloodthirsty—-!
He couldn't fight like a man?
Had to sneak into Troy like a snake!
I'm to serve this most cowardly, slimy, cheating—

TALTHYBIUS:
Miss Queen Hecuba,
we ask that you kindly calm yourself down for just a
moment
as we think you *might* be mistaken.
This is *Odysseus* Odysseus.
The man who ordered the building of the Trojan Horse
after being inspired by the great Athena?
The man who wheeled it to the gates of Troy disguised
as a gift?

The man who hid inside with hundreds of other
Greeks
then burst forth and destroyed the city of Troy in a
great rain of triumph and glory?
That Odysseus.

HECUBA: *(To the* CHORUS*)*
Weep for me, women of Troy.
For I have drawn the very worst lot of all.

(THE CIVILIAN *drops* HECUBA *and hoists the two umbrellas,
or the* CHORUS, *for their next 2 lines.)*

CHORUS 1:
But who owns *me?*

CHORUS 2:
And who owns *me!?*

TALTHYBIUS:
Hold on hold on—do I smell smoke?!
Miss Queen Hecuba!
Are your Trojan women *burning* something?

HECUBA:
That's Cassandra, property of your king.
She carries with her a torch.
Here she comes.

THE CIVILIAN:
ENTER CASSANDRA!

(THE CIVILIAN *lights a camping lantern and becomes*
CASSANDRA.*)*

(CASSANDRA *performs a 1950s rock love song, something
like* Today I Met The Boy I'm Gonna Marry *as sung by
Darlene Love, entirely to herself, swaying, losing herself,
carrying the lantern around the space. She sings with the
internal joy of a madwoman.)*

HECUBA:
Cassandra.

(CASSANDRA, *not hearing* HECUBA, *continues singing.*)

HECUBA:
Cassandra.

(CASSANDRA *sings.*)

HECUBA: *(New tactic)*
Uh—Talthybius, kind herald—

(CASSANDRA *sings.*)

HECUBA:
Won't you allow me a moment with my daughter?

(CASSANDRA *sings.*)

HECUBA:
On this, the eve of my daughter's enslavement?

TALTHYBIUS:
We encourage you to take all the time you need with
your loved ones.

(HECUBA *takes* CASSANDRA *aside.*)

HECUBA: *(Measured)*
Cassandra, I know you haven't been *well,*
but *I* need to understand
that *you* understand
the *gravity* of your situation.

CASSANDRA:
Mother?

HECUBA:
Yes?

CASSANDRA:
Troy *won.*

HECUBA:
No, Cassandra. *Greece* won.

CASSANDRA:
No no no no no think about it:
The Greeks who fell in Troy

died alone in a foreign land, miles from their families,
leaving thousands of widows and orphans in a sea of
despair and confusion.
Dead men forever nameless— and for *what*?
For *Helen?*
Helen's little domestic *dispute*?
It's *insane*, mother! *INSANE!*
But Troy?
Troy fought for *Troy.*
Trojans died defending their homeland.
Fought by day, returned to their loving wives and
children by night.
These pleasures the Greeks forfeited.
My brothers, Hector and Paris, came to violent ends,
yes, but mother—
had the Greeks not attacked, who would remember
how brave my brothers were?
Who would have remembered *us*, even?!
All war is madness, yes,
but when war is *forced* upon you,
when you die a hero,
you reign triumphant for all eternity even in the face of
defeat!

HECUBA:
Cassandra,
slow down.

CASSANDRA: *(Bursting with excitement)*
I can't Mother, I'm too excited!
I'm to be given to the king, Mother!
And then—
And then—
AND THEN—

HECUBA:
And then what?

CASSANDRA: *(Giggling)*
Shhhh….

HECUBA:
What?

CASSANDRA: *(Bursting to tell)*
Shhh Mother, don't tell.

HECUBA:
Don't tell what?

CASSANDRA: *(Whispering)*
He's going to die, Mother.

HECUBA:
Who?

CASSANDRA:
Agamemnon!
I see it all so clearly:
As soon as I get there he'll be murdered where he
sleeps.

HECUBA:
Shhh!
By *who*?

CASSANDRA:
Who else? His own wife!

HECUBA:
I don't believe that.

CASSANDRA:
I know! But it doesn't matter what you believe, Mother.
It is written.
There he is, bleeding out upon his silken sheets.
And then there's me, hounded naked through the
echoing marble hallways of the shamed and lowly
house of Atreus!

HECUBA:
You?

CASSANDRA:
Of course me!
You don't think that wife of his'll spare *me*, do you?
She'll catch me and kill me and open up my body and
drain my blood like a deer's carcass and toss me to the
dogs!
Thus always to discarded meat!

HECUBA:
I don't believe it, it's all too horrible, I just don't believe
it—

CASSANDRA:
I know, I know, I know you don't believe it—
but don't worry, Mother.
My father and brothers' blood *will be avenged.*

TALTHYBIUS:
Uh, Miss Cassandra?

CASSANDRA: *(Suddenly vicious)*
WHAT.

TALTHYBIUS:
Uh… Although we recognize that your mental health
is compromised,
we *do* ask that you *not* make threats against your new
Greek masters.
Okay?

CASSANDRA: *(Rageful, at* TALTHYBIUS*)*
SYCOPHANT!

TALTHYBIUS:
Excuse me?

CASSANDRA:
Bootlicker of murderers, rapists and tyrants!

TALTHYBIUS:
I'm…only doing my job.

CASSANDRA:
And that makes you worse than any of them!
You caused this suffering in Troy, *herald! YOU!*

TALTHYBIUS:
Me?
I didn't kill anyone, Miss Cassandra.
I'm the *messenger.*

CASSANDRA:
You killed them *all,* messenger!

TALTHYBIUS:
How dare you!
I am a peaceful man!

CASSANDRA:
HA!
The very *moment* you looked away from the murder of
a single innocent Trojan,
You, messenger, became responsible for the murders of
them all!

TALTHYBIUS: *(Offended at first, then internally)*
But I…I can't be responsible, I can't possibly…

CASSANDRA:
(Suddenly emotionally and physically fatigued)
Yeah right okay alright I'm done, I'm done, I'm done.

TALTHYBIUS: *(A moment of panicked introspection)*
I—I'm only following orders…

CASSANDRA:
Where's the ship, let's go, I'm done, where's the ship.

(HECUBA collapses.)

CASSANDRA:
Oh Mother!
Don't cry! We will all be together again soon.
It's all going to be alright, don't you see?
I will be the *ruin* of the house of Atreus.

And then together we'll all sink triumphant into happy death!

THE CIVILIAN:
Exit Cassandra and Talthybius.

(THE CIVILIAN *tosses the now off lantern, clipboard and papers haphazardly.*)

(*She hoists the two umbrellas as the* CHORUS.)

CHORUS 1:
Queen Hecuba?

CHORUS 2:
Your majesty?

CHORUS 1:
Are you…dead?

CHORUS 2:
Was Cassandra's fate the coup de gras?

CHORUS 1:
The final blow?

CHORUS 2:
Do you need help, oh queen?

HECUBA:
Leave me here.
Don't make me get up.
I want to lie here.
Until my body breaks down
and becomes a part
of the ground.
And one day,
many years from now,
people will dance on me,
not knowing.
(*Small beat*)
She was once a little girl.
I raised her. Fretted, worried, wondered.

And now,
to have her taken by strangers—
It doesn't make sense.

THE CIVILIAN:
Queen Hecuba?

HECUBA:
Yes?

THE CIVILIAN:
If you are looking for sense,
perhaps we are not the species for you.

(THE CIVILIAN *looks at the stroller and blue puffy coat again
and comes close to falling apart, close to keening again. But
instead, speaks.)*

THE CIVILIAN:
Oh God.
(Beat)
"Oh God?"
What a waste of breath that word is, "God".
What a joke, what a hilarious song and dance that is,
God!
Knock knock?
Who's there?
God!
God who?
God who is a gigantic lie to keep vast swaths of
humanity compliant for when the human monsters
and their machines arrive on their shores to slit their
ignorant throats and bash their gullible brains in and
explode them into a million pieces.

(THE CIVILIAN *hoists the broken umbrellas for* CHORUS.)

CHORUS 1:
If only we hadn't let that horse in.

CHORUS 2:
If only we ignored it.

CHORUS 1:
This is our own fault.

CHORUS 2:
But *of course* we took in the wooden horse.

CHORUS 1:
I eagerly grabbed a rope myself and pulled.

CHORUS 2:
We all did.

CHORUS 1:
Because you can't go through life mistrusting
everything.

CHORUS 2:
You can't assume everyone's out to murder you.

CHORUS 1:
So of course we opened the doors for the horse.

CHORUS 1:
If only we hadn't!
If only we hadn't!

CHORUS 2:
Oh I remember that night so well.
The horse inlaid with so much gold it twinkled in the
moonlight.
I'd never seen anything so strange and beautiful.

CHORUS 1:
If only we hadn't!

CHORUS 2:
Twenty feet wide and thirty-five feet tall!
It sat atop great smooth wheels,
with thick ropes dangling at the horse's broad chest,
Ropes right there,
begging us to grab it and pull it in.

CHORUS 1:
If only we hadn't!

CHORUS 2:
"A gift!" someone shouted, I remember.
"A concession from the Greeks!"
"The war is over!" someone shouted, I remember.
"War is over! War is over! War is over!"

CHORUS 1:
If only, if only, if only!

CHORUS 2:
And despite the late hour, every Trojan from every
family poured forth from every house.
I'd never seen such joy!
Children dancing at midnight!
Young girls leaping and twirling,
Women jumping into each other's arms,
Men hollering and hooting and stomping out a
rhythm.
Music rising from every corner of Troy.

CHORUS 1:
But amid the raucous celebration—

CHORUS 2:
The horse
quietly
opened up—

CHORUS 1:
Gently,
like the mechanical music box I had as a girl.

CHORUS 2:
And out—

CHORUS 1:
—they—

CHORUS 2:
—came.

CHORUS 1:
Wave upon wave upon wave of Greeks soldiers.

Steely in armor, swords sharp and glittering in the
moonlight.

CHORUS 2:
Run Trojans!

CHORUS 1:
How did they all *fit* in there?

CHORUS 2:
Mothers— grab your children! Your dresses cannot
shield them!

CHORUS 1:
How cruel to catch us off guard.
To wake us from our beds.
To ambush us undressed and unarmed.

CHORUS 2:
What a trick.

CHORUS 1:
What a cheat.

CHORUS 2:
What came next:

CHORUS 1:
Bloody floors.

CHORUS 2:
Bloody walls.

CHORUS 1:
Bloody beds.

CHORUS 2:
Bloody sheets.

CHORUS 1:
Bloody hands.

CHORUS 2:
Bloody nails.

CHORUS 1:
Bloody hair.

CHORUS 2:
Bloody wails—

CHORUS 1:
—in the bloody air.

CHORUS 2:
Queen Hecuba, look!
Andromache is coming!

CHORUS 1:
Andromache is coming!

THE CIVILIAN:
Andromache…

(THE CIVILIAN *goes to the blue puffy coat and gently lifts it, carries it to the stroller and straps it back in.*)

THE CIVILIAN:
Andromache.
Only an unnamed good wife and mother.
Good nose, good breasts, good listener, all that.
No name needed.

(THE CIVILIAN *slowly walks the stroller around the stage, like she did at the top.*)

(*The stroller/coat is now* ANDROMACHE. *She is stone cold, direct, biting, angry and accusing.*)

ANDROMACHE:
Hecuba.

HECUBA:
Daughter-in-law.

ANDROMACHE:
Hector is dead, I'm not your daughter-in-law anymore.

HECUBA:
Well then what are you?

ANDROMACHE:
I'm the messenger.

HECUBA:
The messenger?
You're not the messenger, you're my dead son's wife—

ANDROMACHE:
Oh no dear gramma.
I *am* the messenger.
And before I am dragged onto a Greek ship,
before they enslave me and my little Astyanax,
The messenger will give you a message.

HECUBA:
I won't hear it!
I don't deserve this!
There's no more tragic figure than I!

ANDROMACHE:
Here's the message: This is your fault.

HECUBA:
My *fault?*

ANDROMACHE:
You *made* him.
Paris.
He crawled out of your poison womb.

HECUBA:
But I can't be held responsible for—

ANDROMACHE:
For what?
The Judgment of Paris?

HECUBA:
Stop!

ANDROMACHE:
The big party on Mount Olympus?

HECUBA:
Enough!

ANDROMACHE:
The impromptu beauty contest?
"Paris! So sexy, foreign, big and tall!
Who's the prettiest goddess of us all?"
What kind of mother are you?

HECUBA:
A *good* mother.

ANDROMACHE:
HA HA! A good mother?! *Good?*
Who raised her boy to steal a woman out of her
bedroom in the middle of the night?
He wanted her so he took her?
Good mothering, Hecuba, good!
And not just any woman—the wife of the king of
Sparta! Helen!

HECUBA:
Don't you speak her name!
You've got it all wrong! Helen *seduced* my son!

ANDROMACHE:
Spare me.
So you can stop your hapless victim song.
The Trojan War is *your* war.

HECUBA:
I was a *good* mother.

ANDROMACHE:
And I got another message for you:
Your youngest girl, Polyxena, is dead.

HECUBA:
No, no, she's not dead, she has a job.
She's watching over the grave of Achilles——

ANDROMACHE:
She was *sacrificed* to Achilles.

Throat slit ear to ear, I saw it myself.
I—I…I wrapped her in a blanket.
Anyway, she's one of the lucky ones.

HECUBA:
Don't say that!
Where's there's life, there's hope!
That's what people say, isn't it? Where there's life
there's hope?

ANDROMACHE: *(Laughing)*
Where there's life, there's hope?
You naive Trojan buffoon!
There's no hope here!
Living this life is *worse* than death, don't you see that?!

(ANDROMACHE *addresses the next speech to a garbage can
lid representing Hektor's shield.*)

ANDROMACHE:
Oh Hector, my beautiful, steady, pure, *manly* husband.
I did everything *right*, Hector.
I never lied or cheated or snuck out at night!
I didn't drink or smoke or–or–or eat sugar, even!
I didn't nag, gossip, talk back!
I cleaned, washed, folded, cooked, *baked*!
And I did it happily because—
—because when you'd wrap your thick arms around
me,
pulled me to you,
when I buried my face in your neck
and inhaled you…
When I climbed on top of you,
night after night, boarding your great *heaving*
warship—
And now you're gone, Hector.
And I walk the earth
a stinking carcass.

HECUBA:
I knew love, too you know! I knew *lust*!
My dead husband Priam, now *there* was a man!

ANDROMACHE: *(Laughing bitterly)*
Old Priam?! *Really?*
My skin *burns* at the very *thought* of Hector,
the ghost of him possesses me daily, even in death!
Even as a slave to *Neoptolemus*.
That ginger little fuck.
Oh…
All is lost, all is lost.
Well, almost.
(To the coat in the stroller)

ANDROMACHE:
I still have Astyanax.
My fierce little boy.
Strong and fearless, like his daddy.
Wherever we're taken,
We're taken together.

THE CIVILIAN:
Enter Talthybius.

(THE CIVILIAN *becomes* TALTHYBIUS, *grabbing the clipboard and papers, standing on the stool. He is noticeably less confident now.)*

TALTHYBIUS:
Andromache, wife of Hector?
We ask for a moment of your time.
We have some…news.

ANDROMACHE:
News?

TALTHYBIUS:
Yes, news.
Uh.
Well, it seems…that…

The Greeks voted and, uh, well…
the vote was unanimous.

ANDROMACHE:
What vote was unanimous?

TALTHYBIUS:
Just a vote they had, another vote, nothing out of the
ordinary, Greeks vote about everything really.

ANDROMACHE:
This vote was about *what?*
Are we to be separated? Is that it?
Astyanax is to have a different master than me?

TALTHYBIUS:
Uh, no, uh.
The thing is,
no Greek wants to be his master,
none will claim him.
They're worried if they take him,
he'll grow up to avenge his father's death.
Even I'll admit Hector was a great warrior, really *really*
great.
And if he were *my* father, why, I'd want to avenge him
too,
so I get their concerns.

ANDROMACHE:
What do you mean?

TALTHYBIUS:
I mean I—
I know you think I'm only a heartless middleman,
without feelings, without a soul, without a life of my
own.
But I need you to understand that—that—that I do
have those things, I do!
But I am only the *messenger* here, the messenger!
I have a job to do!
I don't wanna get killed myself!

I—I have a family too, I have children, a boy and a girl!
I am only following orders!
(A silence)
The boy must die.
(Another silence)
He's to be
flung
from the walls of Troy.
The highest wall,
they said.
(Another silence)
Better you let him go now, Miss Andromache.
You have no power here, believe me, you don't.
You are just one woman.
They are an army.
If you don't do this *gracefully*—
if you fight or try to kill him yourself—
Then– then they won't allow a burial!
They'll throw him and *leave him* for the birds and the
beasts.
And you don't want that, do you?

(ANDROMACHE *grabs the stroller and runs in that original
stage circle from the top.)*

(TALTHYBIUS *stops her, grappling violently. [As a solo
performance of course, this chase scene can be executed
creatively.])*

(ANDROMACHE *keens as she runs ever faster.)*

(*An explosion is heard, the same from the top.)*

(ANDROMACHE *comes to an abrupt halt as* THE CIVILIAN's
own story breaks in, substituting for ANDROMACHE's *final
lament.)*

THE CIVILIAN:
And now—a massive crash,
a ball of stinging dust
and everything is brown and silent.

And suddenly I am...lighter?
Because
he is gone.
Whisked from my arms as lightly as a dandelion seed
in the breeze.
And there–
his blue puffy winter coat...
Lying there, away from me.
Bright,
so I can spot him.

ANDROMACHE:
Take him.

(*Silence a moment*)

(ANDROMACHE *kneels before the stroller, gently turns it around, and pushes it off the stage.*)

ANDROMACHE:
(*Speaking up to the ceiling and the gods*)
In all your whimsy,
Your playful grapple for power,
Your beauty contest,
You gods blithely murder an innocent child,
And the mother who could not save him.

THE CIVILIAN:
Exit Andromache.

(*Silence a moment*)

THE CIVILIAN:
What's the point of this?

(*Silence another moment, as* THE CIVILIAN *hoists the 2 umbrellas to perform* CHORUS.)

(THE CIVILIAN *stands between* CHORUS *1 and 2.*)

CHORUS 2:
What's the *point*?

CHORUS 1:
How can you ask that? You think there's a *point*?

CHORUS 2:
You think there's meaning to all this?

CHORUS 1:
You think there's some great logical narrative to the universe?

CHORUS 2:
That this happened for a reason?

CHORUS 1:
Maybe.
Maybe everything happens for a reason.

CHORUS 2:
If you believe that
you're stupider than I thought.

CHORUS 1:
All is entropy.
Cruel randomness.

CHORUS 2:
Couldn't humans make it better?
If we all tried together? Couldn't we?

CHORUS 1:
Of course!

THE CIVILIAN:
But they won't!

CHORUS 2:
Why not?!

CHORUS 1:
Because.

THE CIVILIAN:
Then what will I do?

CHORUS 1:
Isn't it obvious?
The show must go on.

CHORUS 2:
The show must go on.

THE CIVILIAN:
But if it can't?

CHORUS 1:
It must.

(*A small silence*)

(THE CIVILIAN *locates and puts on a destroyed bicycle
helmet. This is* MENELAUS.)

THE CIVILIAN:
Enter Menelaus,
King of Sparta, husband to Helen, little brother to king
Agamemnon,
an eternal second fiddle.

MENELAUS:
(*Pent up, growly, through clenched teeth*)
Hecuba. Where is she?

HECUBA:
Who?

MENELAUS:
(*Super repressed and measured in his macho anger*)
Helen.
I got
a hundred men here
to haul her away
and watch me
as I
beat her
to death.

HECUBA:
Oh *her*.
You came all the way to Troy just to kill Helen?

MENELAUS:
Yes. Yes I did.

HECUBA:
Wonderful.
Do you mind if I watch?
Do you mind if I help?

MENELAUS:
I'm gonna do it myself.
And I'll do it, too.

HECUBA:
No one's doubting you.

MENELAUS:
I mean, I *will* beat her to death.

HECUBA:
Good.

MENELAUS:
The minute I see her.
I mean,
if not here in Troy, then…
At home in Sparta.
You know,
In the privacy
of our own
home.
(Small beat. Defensive)
What?

HECUBA:
She's not even here yet and you're bending to her will.
But what luck, here she comes!
Don't look into your wife's eyes, Menelaus.
That woman can ruin a man with a single look.

(THE CIVILIAN *tosses off* MENELAUS.)

(THE CIVILIAN *locates a long stretch of chain and wears
it around her wrists, held out in front of her body, like
handcuffs, representative of* HELEN OF TROY.)

THE CIVILIAN:
Enter Helen.
Helen: The who, the what, the how and the why of The
Trojan War.
The most beautiful woman who ever lived? Perhaps.
But beauty is only a genetic mishap,
no more likely than any other physical mutation.
More importantly, Helen is ambiguous—ambiguity
becomes Helen.
Rape victim or seductress?
Faithful or disloyal?
Prisoner or guard?
Predator or prey?

(HELEN *is steady, stoic, disturbingly measured, as described
above she becomes ambiguity.*)

HELEN:
Menelaus.

MENELAUS: *(Dumbstruck and horny)*
Huh–huh–huh—Hel hel hel—

HELEN: *(Calm, but steadfast)*
Well?
What are you waiting for, husband?
I stand before you in chains.
If you're here to kill me,
then kill me.

MENELAUS:
Uh…well.
No. I mean yeah.
I mean—I'm definitely here to kill you.

HELEN:
Alright, then.

(MENELAUS *acts like he is about to kill* HELEN, *but he can't do it.*)

HELEN:
What's wrong, husband?

(Beat)

HELEN:
Can't you do it?

(Beat. MENELAUS *can't do it.)*

HELEN:
Alright.
May I take this moment to speak?

HECUBA:
No! Don't let her talk! We all know how she operates!
She'll talk herself right back into your bed, you
spineless idiot!
Stab her! Stone her! Kill her!

HELEN: *(Strangely serene)*
Only a few words, Hecuba.
(Beat)
Thank you.
I did not leave you, Menelaus.
I was kidnapped.
I did not seduce Paris.
Paris won me in a contest—you know the one.
The beauty contest.
Important work, judging that contest, important work.
So what could I do?
Paris came to Sparta.
Came into my room while I slept—he and Aphrodite
herself.
They grabbed me awake by my ankles, yanked me out
of bed.

So what could I do?
I tried, husband, I tried.
I clung to the bedposts, dragged my nails across the
bedroom floor.
"You can't just *take* me!" I said.
But he can. He's a man. And she can. She is a goddess.
So what could I do?

MENELAUS:
Paris was soon killed.
So why did you stay in Troy?
Why didn't you come back to me?

HELEN:
I tried to escape nightly.
I repelled the battlements on ropes and sheets,
sometimes with my bare hands.
But Hecuba was always there.
She never let me leave.
Because she knew if I left,
I'd tell the world that Paris kidnapped me.
So
what
could
I
do?

MENELAUS:
I don't know.
I—I should still kill you.

HELEN:
Alright.
(*She is surreptitiously unwinding the chain from her
wrists.*)
But understand: I had no free will.
I had no free will with you.
I had no free will with Paris.
And, of course, I have no free will where I stand now.

I wouldn't know what free will was
if you gifted me all of it in the world.
(*She drops the chain.*)

MENELAUS:
Uh huh.
Well, uh, we can just…talk about this at home.
Let's get on the ship and go—

(THE CIVILIAN *tosses everyone down and hoists the 2*
CHORUS *umbrellas.*)

CHORUS 1:
Cross-examination time, liar.

CHORUS 2:
Your story doesn't track.

CHORUS 1:
Why would the goddesses hold a beauty contest?

CHORUS 2:
Goddesses aren't insecure like us—*they're goddesses.*

CHORUS 1:
And why would Aphrodite have to *physically* take you?

CHORUS 2:
Couldn't she just make you appear wherever she
wanted?

CHORUS 1:
And are you saying you were *in no way* attracted to
Paris?

CHORUS 2:
The big, strong, *rippling* Paris of Troy?

CHORUS 1:
The sweaty, musky, *masculine* Paris of Troy?

CHORUS 2:
The delicious, virile, *thirsty* Paris of Troy?

CHORUS 1:
Also did anyone *witness* this kidnapping?

CHORUS 2:
Did you scream?

CHORUS 1:
No one in Sparta reported hearing any screams that
night.

CHORUS 2:
And are you saying you were *completely* happily
married to Menelaus, here? He with the sex drive of a
kumquat?

CHORUS 1:
And about your alleged escapes—
If you were so miserable why didn't you just tie that
chain around your neck and end it all?

CHORUS 2:
That would have made *quite* a political statement, don't
you think?

CHORUS 1:
You had the free will to do that, did you not?

CHORUS 2:
Why?

CHORUS 1:
Why?!

CHORUS 2:
WHY?!

HECUBA:
QUIET!
There was one night…
There was one night…
I remember…
The wind outside smelled of death and decay.
I came to Helen in her perfumed rooms,

I remember…
She was nestled in her finery—Paris' finery.
There she was fat and happy atop a mountain of food
and wine and silks and jewels.
I stood in the doorway, I remember,
And I held open the door.
And I said:
Go Helen.
Go.
You are free to go. Go back to Sparta and end this.

(Beat)

HELEN: *(Calmly)*
Well
that
is
simply
not
true.

HECUBA: *(Enraged)*
GRRRRAAAAHHH!
LIAR!
Stab her! Stone her! Kill her!

MENELAUS:
Enough!
Helen.
The ship.
Now.

THE CIVILIAN:
Exit Menelaus and Helen.

(THE CIVILIAN *then hoists both umbrellas for the final
Choral ode.)*

CHORUS 1:
Is this what you wanted, you gods?

THE CIVILIAN:
Don't ask, they don't listen.

CHORUS 2:
Was all our worship a complete waste of time?

THE CIVILIAN:
Don't ask, they don't listen.

CHORUS 1:
This is the world for you, gods?

THE CIVILIAN:
Don't ask, don't ask…

CHORUS 1:
Look! Who comes?
What new horror approaches the corpse of Troy?

(THE CIVILIAN *tosses the umbrellas aside.*)

THE CIVILIAN:
Enter Talthybius.

(TALTHYBIUS *enters, papers in hand, but also cradling the child's blue winter coat.*)

TALTHYBIUS:
(*Struggling to maintain his customer service tone, which has become all but impossible for him:*)
Hello.
Talthybius here. Again.
We, uh, we thank you for standing by.
Um.
I—I'm here because…
I watched as Andromache's ship took her away.
Alone. As was dictated.
And…
Well, as she departed, she howled to me a haunting thing, and…
…and as a messenger, although I am strictly forbidden to act outside my given orders,
regardless of my own personal moral code—

which I *do* have, I do have a moral code, believe it or
not—
I promised to her that I'd grant her final wish,
and see her little boy buried,
snugly, by your hand, if not hers.
So,
here you go.
I even cleaned him for you myself,
which would most certainly get me fired, but…oh well.
Take care, Mom.

THE CIVILIAN:
Exit Talthybius.
Exit Hecuba.
Exit The Chorus.
Leaving only me, and grief, alone.

(THE CIVILIAN *casts the clipboard and papers aside. She
then curls her body around the blue coat.*)

THE CIVILIAN:
If only we hadn't.
If only.
If only.
My little blue boy.
Bright, so I could see him.
Who had only tasted just a moment of life.
But now,
No more.
No best friends.
No school.
No recess.
No baseball.
No soccer.
No birthday parties.
No school plays.
No homework.
No little jeans ripped at the knees.
No new shoes.

No trampolines.
No flirting.
No girls.
No boys.
No break ups.
No cool hair with gel.
No dances.
No late nights laughing.
No phone.
No bike.
No car.
No college.
No summers.
No job.
No beer after work.
No memory.
No pain.

(THE CIVILIAN *looks up to the ceiling and addresses the gods.*)

THE CIVILIAN:
Shame on you.
(*She turns her head and addresses the audience directly.*)
Shame on you.

(THE CIVILIAN *lies on the floor completely, like* HECUBA *at the top, and remains on the floor for the rest of the piece, blue winter coat in arms.*)

THE CIVILIAN:
But I won't get up.
I will lie here.
Until my body breaks down
and becomes a part of the street.
And one day,
many years from now,
people will dance on me,
not knowing.

(Blackout)

END OF PLAY